1950s

Ten Years of Popular SHEET MUSIC BESTSELLERS

DECADE by DECADE

Alfred Music Publishing Co., Inc.
16320 Roscoe Blvd., Suite 100
P.O. Box 10003
Van Nuys, CA 91410-0003

alfred.com

ISBN-10: 0-7390-6021-X
ISBN-13: 978-0-7390-6021-6

Cover photo: © istockphoto / James Group Studios

Contents

ALL I HAVE TO DO IS DREAM

Words and Music by
BOUDLEAUX BRYANT

* Original recording down ½ step in E♭.

All I Have to Do Is Dream - 4 - 1

5

6

ev - er I want you,___ all I have to do   is   dream,_____

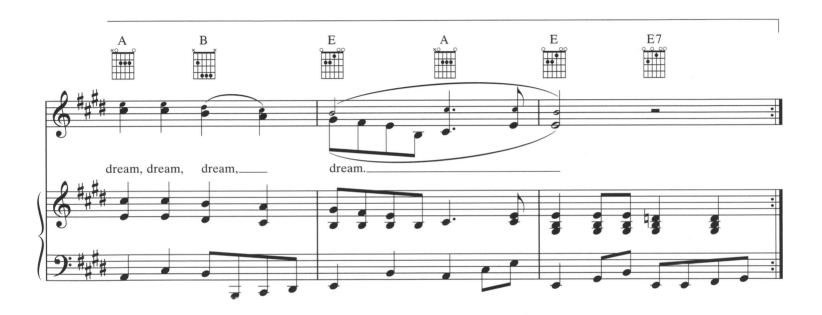

dream, dream, dream,_____   dream._____

Repeat ad lib. and fade

all I have to do   is   dream,_____   dream, dream,   dream,_____

THE BEST IS YET TO COME

Music by
CY COLEMAN

Lyrics by
CAROLYN LEIGH

Refrain:

Out of the tree of life___ I just picked me a plum,___

you came a-long and ev-'ry-thing's start-in' to hum;___

still it's a real good bet___ the best is yet to come.___

The best is yet to come___ and, babe, won't it be fine,___ you think you've seen the sun,___ but you ain't seen it shine.___

Wait till the warm-up's un-der way,___ wait till our lips have met,___ wait till you see that sun-shine day,___ you ain't seen noth-in' yet!

BIRD DOG

Words and Music by
BOUDLEAUX BRYANT

Moderately ♩ = 120

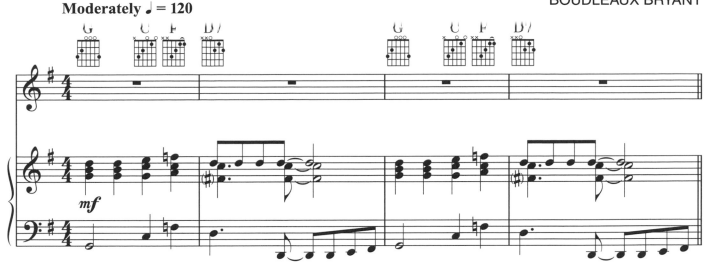

Verse:

1. John-ny is a jok - er, (He's a bird.) a ver-y fun-ny jok - er. (He's a bird.) But
2.3. See additional lyrics

when he jokes my hon - ey, (He's a dog.) his jok-in' ain't so fun - ny. (What a dog.)

Bird Dog - 3 - 1

hunting, you'd bel-ter find a chick-en in-he to your own

own.

Verse 2:
Johnny sings a love song. *(Like a bird.)*
He sings the sweetest love song. *(You ever heard.)*
But when he sings to my gal, *(What a howl.)*
To me he's just a wolf dog. *(On the prowl.)*
Johnny wants to fly away and puppy love my baby.
(He's a bird dog.)
(To Chorus:)

Verse 3:
Johnny kissed the teacher. *(He's a bird.)*
He tiptoed up to reach her. *(He's a bird.)*
Well, he's the teacher's pet now. *(He's a dog.)*
What he wants he can get now. *(What a dog.)*
He even made the teacher let him sit next to my baby.
(He's a bird dog.)
(To Chorus:)

BLUEBERRY HILL

Words and Music by
AL LEWIS, VINCENT ROSE
and LARRY STOCK

Moderately ♩. = 92

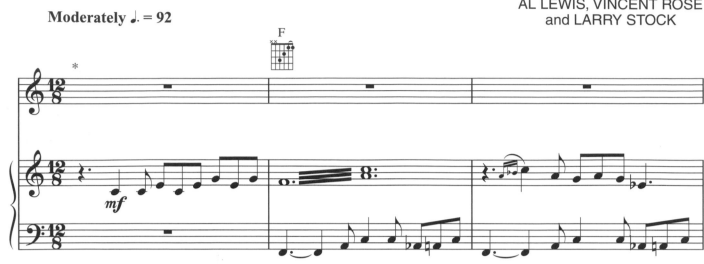

* Original recording in the key of B.

Blueberry Hill - 5 - 1

18

and lin - gered un - til

my dream came

true.   The wind in the

Bridge:

wil - low played   love's sweet mel - o -

BYE, BYE LOVE

Words and Music by
BOUDLEAUX BRYANT
and FELICE BRYANT

Bye, bye,___ love,___ bye, bye,___ hap - pi - ness;___

hel - lo, lone - li - ness.___ I think I'm - a gon - na cry.___

Bye, bye,___ love,___ bye, bye,___ sweet ca - ress;___

Bye, Bye Love - 3 - 1

To Coda ⊕

D   A   E7   A

hel - lo, emp - ti - ness.___ I feel like I___ could die;_____ bye, bye_

E7   A   *Verse:* E7

___ my love,___ good - bye._____

{ 1. There goes my ba - by___
{ 2. I'm through with ro - mance,_

A   E7

with some - one new._____ She sure looks hap - py;___
I'm through with love,_____ I'm through with count - ing___

A   A7   D

I sure am blue._____ She was my ba - by___
the stars a - bove._____ And here's the rea - son___

CRYING IN THE CHAPEL

Slowly, with expression

Words and Music by
ARTIE GLENN

Chorus:

1. You saw me cry-ing in the chap - el;_____ the tears I shed were tears of
some - thing_____ that will put his heart at

joy._____ I know the mean-ing of con - tent - ment,
ease._____ There is on - ly one true an - swer,

Crying in the Chapel - 4 - 1

CHANCES ARE

Words by
AL STILLMAN

Music by
ROBERT ALLEN

EARTH ANGEL
(Will You Be Mine)

Words and Music by
JESSE BELVIN

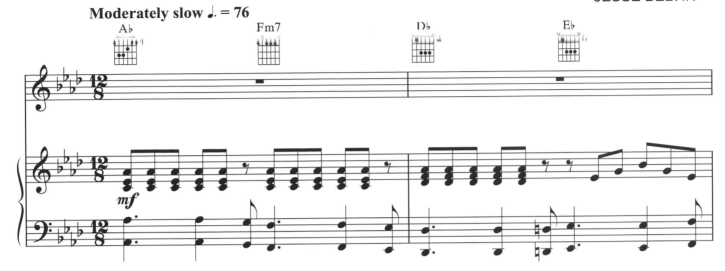

Verse 1:

Earth Angel - 5 - 1

EVERYBODY LOVES TO CHA CHA CHA

Words and Music by
SAM COOKE

Everybody Loves to Cha Cha Cha - 7 - 1

Verse 1:

Verse 4:

4. We kept__ on danc - ing, and was I sur - prised!__ For you

D7 see, af - ter we prac - ticed for a lit - tle while,__ she was **C**

D7 do - ing it bet - ter than me.____ Now,__ my ba - by loves to do__ the **G6** **G**

C cha, cha, cha.__ Ooh, *she loves to do* the cha, cha, cha.__ She likes to, **G**

I COULD HAVE DANCED ALL NIGHT

Lyrics by
ALAN JAY LERNER

Music by
FREDERICK LOEWE

EVERYTHING'S COMING UP ROSES

Lyrics by
STEPHEN SONDHEIM

Music by
JULE STYNE

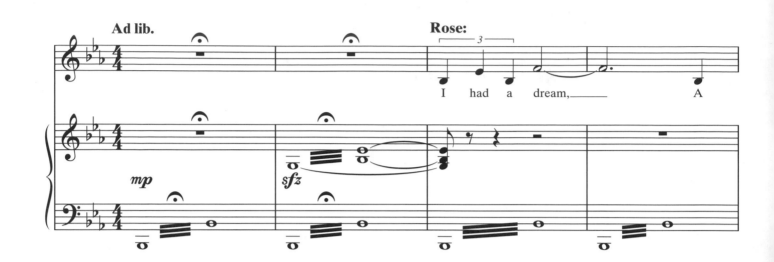

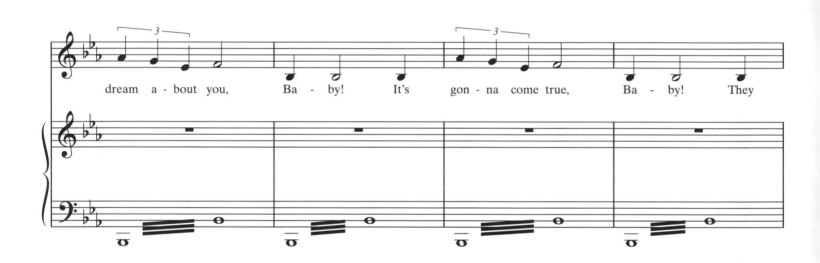

Everything's Coming Up Roses - 8 - 1

Poco allargando

A tempo

Stand the world on its ear!_____ Set it____

_____ spin - ning,_____ That - 'll be just the be -

gin - ning!_____ Cur - tain up,_____ Light the lights,_____

_____ You got noth - ing to hit_____ but the heights!_____ You'll be

56

L'istesso tempo

swell,_____ You'll be great,_____ I can tell,_____ Just you wait!_____ That luck-y star I talk a-bout is due._____ Hon-ey, ev-'ry-thing's com-ing up ros-es for me and for

f

rall.

Everything's Coming Up Roses - 8 - 5

Slowly (♩ = 60)

you!

You can do it,

rit.

p

All you need is a hand,   We   can   do   it,

rit.

rit.

a tempo

Mom-ma is gon-na see to   it!___ Cur - tain   up,___

a tempo

f

___ Light   the   lights,___   We   got   noth - ing   to   hit___   but   the

heights!_____ I can tell,_____ Wait and see!_____

_____ There's the bell,_____ Fol - low me!_____ And

noth - ing's gon - na stop us till we're

through!_____ Hon - ey,

f

L'istesso tempo

Poco meno mosso

ev - 'ry - thing's com - ing up ros - es and daf - fo - dils,

Ev - 'ry - thing's com - ing up sun - shine and San - ta Claus, Ev - 'ry - thing's

gon - na be bright lights and lol - li - pops. Ev - 'ry - thing's com - ing up

ros - es for me and for you.

Everything's Coming Up Roses - 8 - 8

FROM THIS MOMENT ON

Words and Music by
COLE PORTER

From This Moment On - 6 - 4

GREAT BALLS OF FIRE

Words and Music by
OTIS BLACKWELL and JACK HAMMER

Great Balls of Fire - 5 - 1

HEY THERE

Words and Music by
RICHARD ADLER and JERRY ROSS

HOLD ME, THRILL ME, KISS ME

Words and Music by
HARRY NOBLE

Moderately slow ♩. = 80

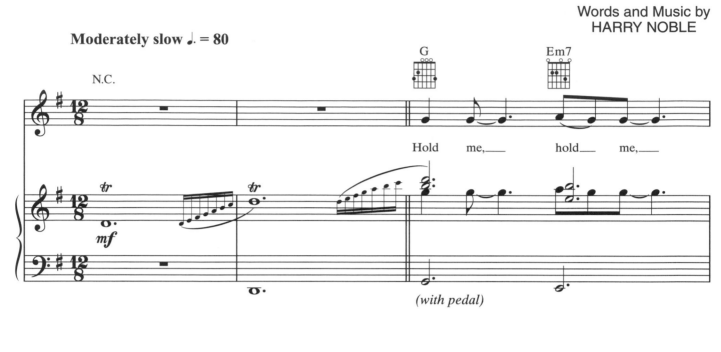

Hold me,___ hold___ me,___

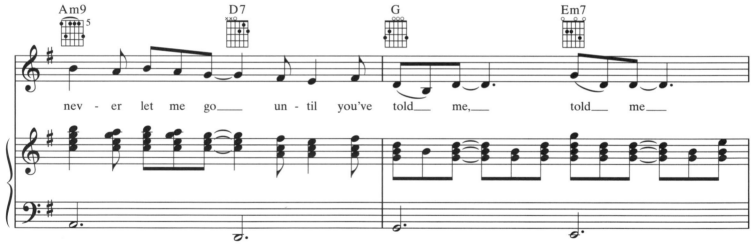

nev- er let me go___ un- til you've told___ me,___ told___ me___

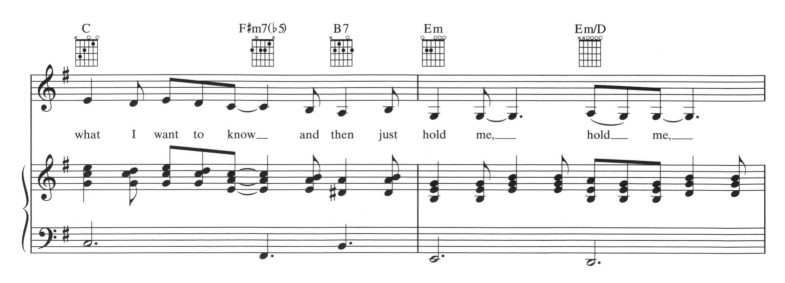

what I want to know___ and then just hold me,___ hold___ me,___

Hold Me, Thrill Me, Kiss Me - 6 - 1

JUST IN TIME

Lyrics by
BETTY COMDEN and
ADOLPH GREEN

Music by
JULE STYNE

82

LIPSTICK ON YOUR COLLAR

Words by
EDNA LEWIS

Music by
GEORGE GOEHRING

LOVE IS A MANY SPLENDORED THING

Lyric by
PAUL FRANCIS WEBSTER

Music by
SAMMY FAIN

LOVE AND MARRIAGE

Lyric by
SAMMY CAHN

Music by
JAMES VAN HEUSEN

Love and Marriage - 3 - 1

MISTY

Words by
JOHNNY BURKE

Music by
ERROLL GARNER

Misty - 3 - 1

MR. LEE

Words and Music by
HEATHER E. DIXON, HELEN GATHERS,
JANICE POUGHT, LAURA E. WEBB
and EMMA RUTH POUGHT

Moderately

One two three

look at Mis-ter Lee, ___ Three four

five look at him jive, Mis-ter

Mr. Lee - 4 - 1

Mr. Lee - 4 - 4

MY SPECIAL ANGEL

Words and Music by
JIMMY DUNCAN

Slowly, with a steady beat

Lyrics:
You are my spe-cial an-gel sent from up a-bove. {The Lord / My fate} smiled down on me and sent an an-gel to love. You are my spe-cial an-gel right from par-a-dise. I know that you're an an-gel; Heav-en's in your

My Special Angel - 2 - 1

ON THE STREET WHERE YOU LIVE

Words by
ALAN JAY LERNER

Music by
FREDERICK LOEWE

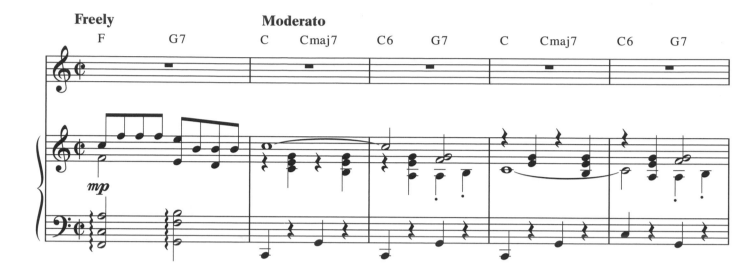

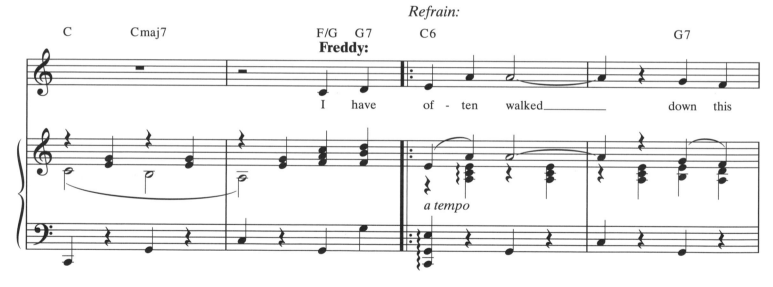

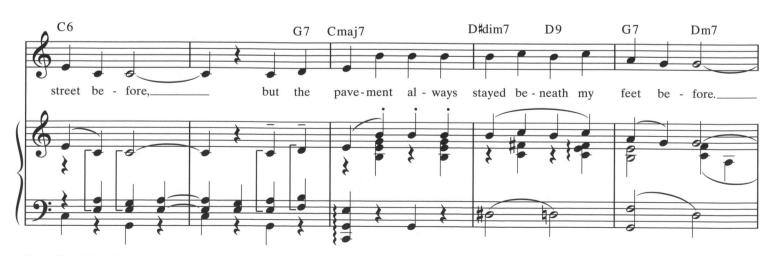

On the Street Where You Live - 4 - 1

ORANGE COLORED SKY

Words and Music by
MILTON DELUGG and
WILLIE STEIN

Orange Colored Sky - 4 - 1

PETER GUNN

By
HENRY MANCINI

Peter Gunn - 3 - 1

(R.H. ad lib. solo if desired)

loco

(We're Gonna) ROCK AROUND THE CLOCK

Words and Music by
MAX C. FREEDMAN and JIMMY DE KNIGHT

Bright rock ♩ = 176

One, two, three o'-clock, four o'-clock rock.

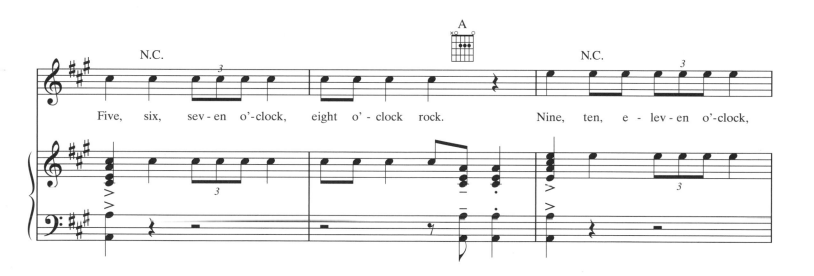

Five, six, sev-en o'-clock, eight o'-clock rock. Nine, ten, e-lev-en o'-clock,

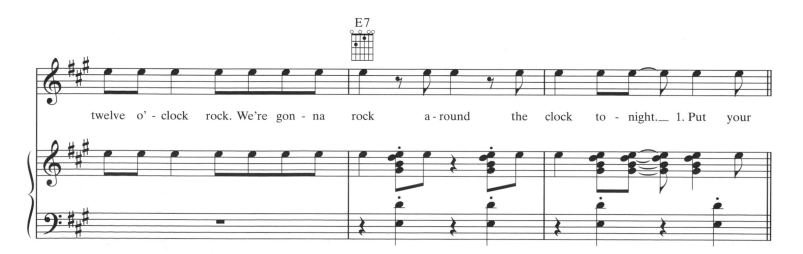

twelve o'-clock rock. We're gon-na rock a-round the clock to-night.__ 1. Put your

(We're Gonna) Rock Around the Clock - 5 - 1

SATIN DOLL

Words and Music by
JOHNNY MERCER, DUKE ELLINGTON
and BILLY STRAYHORN

Satin Doll - 3 - 1

SEE YOU IN SEPTEMBER

Words by
SID WAYNE

Music by
SHERMAN EDWARDS

See You in September - 5 - 1

122

See You in September - 5 - 2

SH-BOOM
(Life Could Be A Dream)

Words and Music by
JAMES KEYES, CLAUDE FEASTER,
CARL FEASTER, FLOYD McRAE and JAMES EDWARDS

Moderately bright

Hey non - ny ding dong a -

lang a - lang a - lang. Boom ba - doh, ___ ba - doo - ba - doo. ___

Life could be a dream, ___ sh - boom, if I could take you up in Par - a - dise up a - bove, sh -

Sh-Boom - 4 - 1

SIXTEEN CANDLES

Words and Music by
LUTHER DIXON and
ALLYSON R. KHENT

Sixteen Candles - 2 - 1

SHAKE, RATTLE AND ROLL

Words and Music by
CHARLES E. CALHOUN

Moderately Bright

VERSE

Get out ___ from that kitch-en and rat-tle those pots and pans, ___

Get out ___ from that kitch-en and rat-tle those pots and pans. ___

Shake, Rattle and Roll - 5 - 1

SIXTEEN TONS

Words and Music by
MERLE TRAVIS

1. Some

Verse:

peo - ple say a man is made out of mud,_____ a
born one_____ morn - in' when the sun did - n't shine._____ I
born one_____ morn - in', it was driz - zl - ing rain._____
see_____ me com - in' bet - ter step a - side,_____ a

poor man's made out of mus - cle and blood.
picked up my shov - el and I walked to the mine, I load - ed
Fight - in' and trou - ble are my mid - dle name._____ I was
lot - ta men did - n't,_____ a lot - ta men died.

Sixteen Tons - 3 - 1

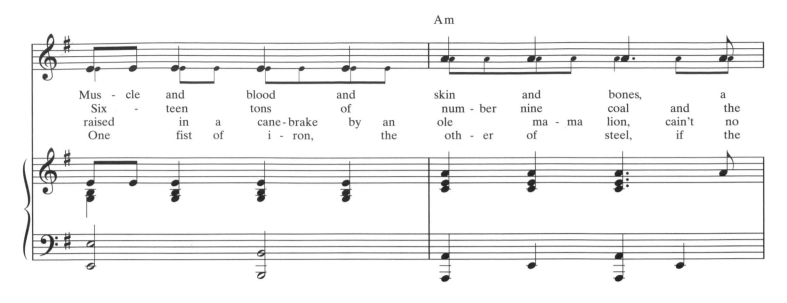

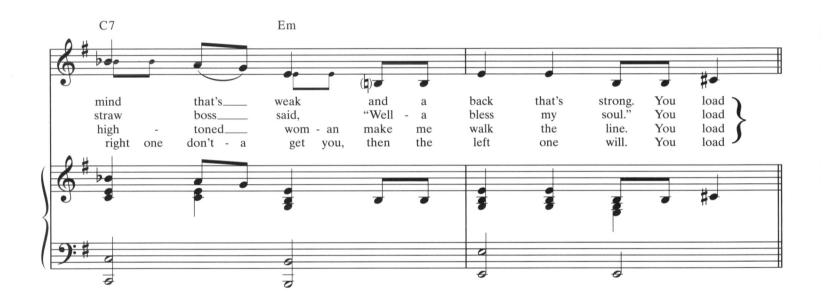

deep - er in debt.___ Saint Pe - ter, don't you call me 'cause I can't go,___ I

owe___ my soul to the com - pa - ny store.___

2. I was
3. I was
4. If you

SLEIGH RIDE

Words by
MITCHELL PARISH

Music by
LEROY ANDERSON

SPLISH SPLASH

Words and Music by
BOBBY DARIN and JEAN MURRAY

SUMMERTIME BLUES

Words and Music by
EDDIE COCHRAN and JERRY CAPEHEART

Moderately fast ♩ = 152

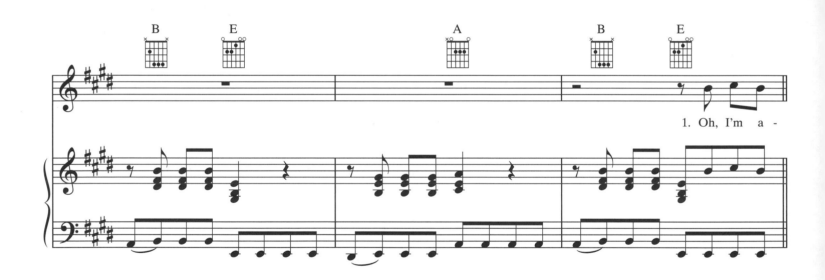

Verse:

gon-na raise a fuss,__ I'm a - gon-na raise a hol-ler,
2.3. *See additional lyrics*

Summertime Blues - 3 - 1

Verse 2:
A-well, my mom and papa told me,
"Son, you gotta make some money,
If you wanna use the car to go a-ridin' next Sunday."
A-well, I didn't go to work, told the boss I was sick.
"Now you can't use the car, 'cause you didn't work a lick."
Sometimes I wonder what I'm a-gonna do,
But there ain't no cure for the summertime blues.

Verse 3:
I'm gonna take two weeks, gonna have a fine vacation.
I'm gonna take my problem to the United Nations.
Well, I called my congessman and he said, quote:
"I'd like to help you, son, but you're too young to vote."
Sometimes I wonder what I'm a-gonna do,
But there ain't no cure for the summertime blues.

A TEENAGER IN LOVE

Words by
DOC POMUS

Music by
MORT SHUMAN

Moderately slow

Chorus:

1. Each time we have a quar-rel it al-most breaks my heart,
2. One day I feel so hap-py; next day I feel so sad.

'cause I am so a-fraid that we will have to part.
I guess I'll learn to take the good with the bad.

Each night I ask the stars up a-bove:

A Teenager in Love - 3 - 1

THANK HEAVEN FOR LITTLE GIRLS

Lyrics by
ALAN JAY LERNER

Music by
FREDERICK LOEWE

Thank Heaven for Little Girls - 6 - 1

THAT'S ENTERTAINMENT!

Words by
HOWARD DIETZ

Music by
ARTHUR SCHWARTZ

Ev-'ry-thing that hap-pens in life_____ can hap-pen in a show._____ You can make them laugh, you can make them cry. An-y-thing, an-y-thing can go._____ The

That's Entertainment! - 5 - 1

Refrain:

clown_____ with his pants fall - ing down,_____ or the
doubt_____ while the ju - ry is out,_____ or the

dance_____ that's a dream of ro - mance,_____ or the
thrill_____ when a they're read - ing the will,_____ or the

scene_____ where the vil - lain is mean;_____ that's
chase_____ for the man with the face;_____ that's

en - ter - tain - ment!_____ The lights_____ on the
en - ter - tain - ment!_____ The dame_____ who is

THREE COINS IN THE FOUNTAIN

Words by
SAMMY CAHN

Music by
JULE STYNE

Three coins in the foun-tain, each one seek-ing hap-pi-ness. Thrown by three hope-ful lov-ers, which one will the foun-tain bless? Three hearts in the

Three Coins in the Fountain - 3 - 1

TILL

English Words by
CARL SIGMAN

Music by
CHARLES DANVERS

Till - 3 - 1

TRUE LOVE

Words and Music by
COLE PORTER

Moderate waltz ♩ = 132

Verse:

Sun - tanned, wind - blown, hon - ey -

moon - ers at last a - lone. Feel - ing

True Love - 3 - 1

Refrain:

far a-bove par; oh, how luck-y we are._____ While I

give to you and you give to me true

love, true love. So, on and on it will

al - ways be true love, true

VOLARE
(Nel Blu, Dipinto Di Blu)

English Lyrics by
MITCHELL PARISH
Original Italian Text by
D. MODUGNO and F. MIGLIACCI

Music by
DOMENICO MODUGNO

Moderately

Volare - 4 - 1

WAKE UP LITTLE SUSIE

Words and Music by
BOUDLEAUX BRYANT
and FELICE BRYANT

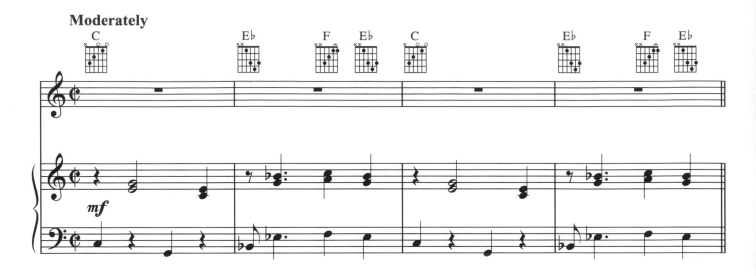

Wake up, Lit - tle Su - sie,___ wake up.

Wake up, Lit - tle Su - sie,___ wake up.

We've / The

Wake Up Little Susie - 4 - 1

WALKIN' MY BABY BACK HOME

Words and Music by
FRED AHLERT and ROY TURK

WHATEVER LOLA WANTS
(Lola Gets)

(Cue:) **LOLA:** And do like Lola tells you to do.

Words and Music by
RICHARD ADLER and JERRY ROSS

Whatever Lola Wants - 3 - 1

WHEN I FALL IN LOVE

Words by
EDWARD HEYMAN

Music by
VICTOR YOUNG

Slowly, with much feeling ♩ = 84

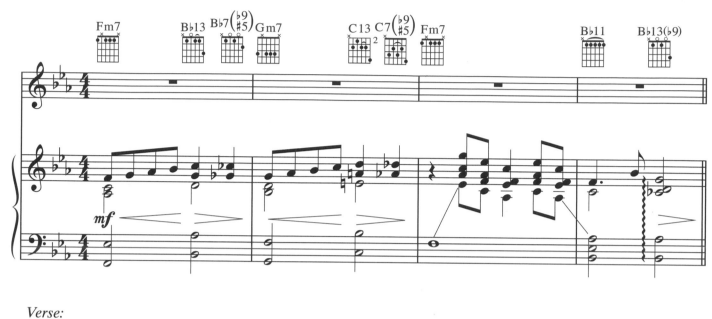

Verse:

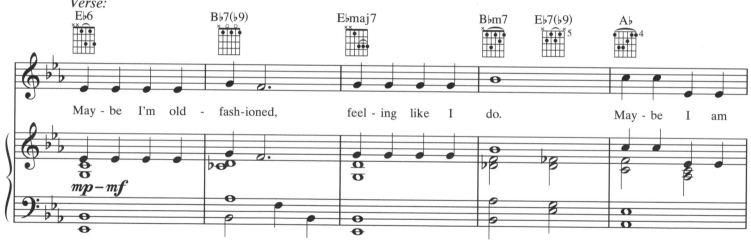

May - be I'm old - fash-ioned, feel - ing like I do. May - be I am

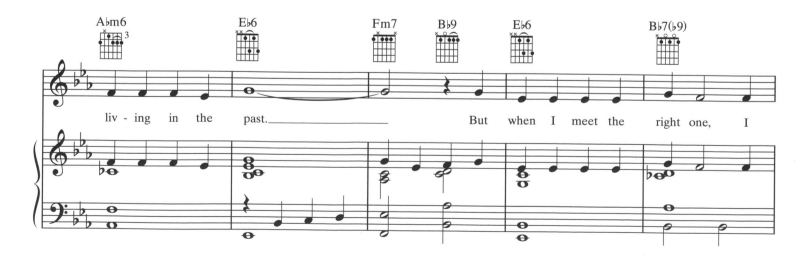

liv - ing in the past._____ But when I meet the right one, I

When I Fall in Love - 3 - 1

WHOLE LOTTA SHAKIN' GOIN' ON

Words and Music by
DAVID WILLIAMS

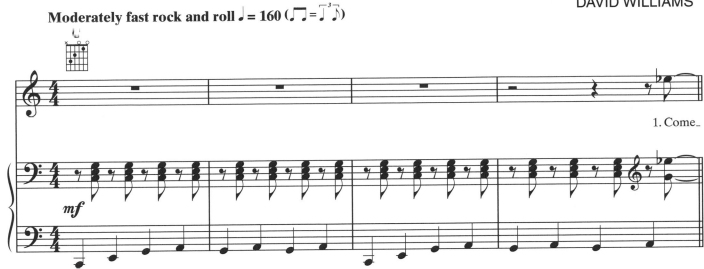

Whole Lotta Shakin' Goin' On - 5 - 1

Piano solo:

Verse 2:
Well, I said come along, my baby, we got chicken in the corn.
Woo-huh, come along, my baby, really got the bull by the horn.
We ain't fakin', whole lotta shakin' goin' on.
(To Chorus:)

Verse 4:
Well, I said come along, my baby, we got chicken in the barn,
whose barn, what barn, my barn.
Come along, my baby, really got the bull by the horn.
We ain't fakin', whole lotta shakin' goin' on.

Chorus 2:
(Spoken:)
Easy now. Shake.
Ah, shake it, baby.
Yeah, you can shake it one time for me.
(Sung:)
Yeah-huh-huh-ha-ha, come along, my baby,
Whole lotta shakin' goin' on.
(To Chorus 3:)

WHO'S SORRY NOW?

Words by
BERT KALMAR and HARRY RUBY

Music by
TED SNYDER

learn - ing to smile.＿＿＿＿＿
just how it feels.＿＿＿＿＿

Who's sor - ry now?

Who's sor - ry now? Whose heart is ach - ing for break - ing each

vow? Who's sad and blue? Who's cry - ing too?

Just like I cried o - ver you.＿＿＿＿＿ Right to the

Who's Sorry Now? - 3 - 2

You Send Me

Words and Music by
SAM COOKE

You Send Me - 5 - 1

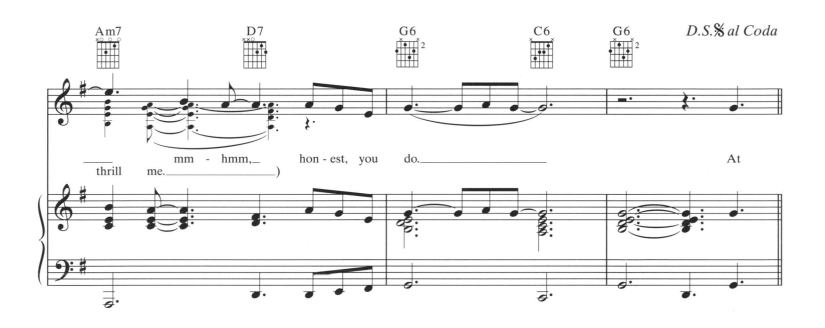

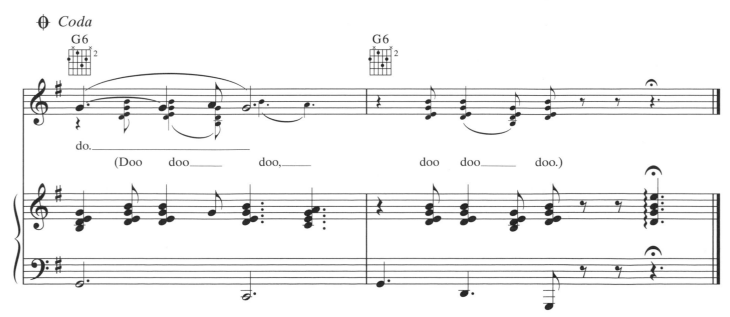

YOUR CHEATIN' HEART

Words and Music by
HANK WILLIAMS

Chorus: